*"November Da[illegible]
collection of bea[illegible]
will not soon lea[illegible] ritual dance
and witness, ghosts of bone and skin, identity rippling into waves crashing into colonial boundaries. Ancestor poems demanding recognition and equity for the ongoing genocide built upon false histories inked in blood and tears."*

- S.A. Griffin, author of ***Pandemic Soul Music***, publisher and editor, ***Catching Fire: The Los Angeles Wildfires January 2025***

"To read Kim Shuck's work is not merely to encounter the singular voice of an acknowledged master of the form but to feel oneself in the presence of a force more powerful than poetry, older than lyric or image or line. Grounded in a precision of objects, prickling with Shuck's spare, pared-down syntax, rooted in the rhythm of the pulse, the poems collected in November Dance Shirt bring to mind Shuck's basket and beadwork: each part deceptive in its simplicity and necessary to the whole."

- Marya Hornbacher, NYT Bestselling author of ***Wasted***, Saints and Sinners LGBTQ+ Poetry Winner 2026 and author of the forthcoming **Solo** (Cardinal/Hachette 2027.)

"Tumbling into dream, perhaps an ancestral labyrinth woven of epiphany, November dance shirt escorts readers into reckonings where memory becomes spirit guide, a torch through the wounds. "Wind that sings through/stones there are/stairways in the woods," Kim Shuck's poems breathe such pathways and shadow dances, as each poem transmutes, unbecomes then regenerates the way all November seasons summon us to do. In this tender collection, Kim Shuck's imagery and diction is palpable, relevant and often conveys two messages at once. Traditional writing tools like punctuation cannot survive when poets walk barefoot through the wounds, when words return home -- to light and shadow patterns that define the anatomy of human suffering. Step into the harvests of Shuck's verse, where thoughts become weapons, where November motifs teach us that transformation, healing, and regrowth is a tight rope we walk between willingness and resistance."

-K.R. Morrison. moon witch, poet, educator, author of ***Cauldrons,*** (PaperPress Books, 2022)

November Dance Shirt

by

Kim Shuck

COLLAPSE PRESS

This book is the twelfth publication by
COLLAPSE PRESS
www.collapsepress.com

ISBN: 979-8-9898579-8-2

On The Cover: Red Legged Frog by Kim Shuck
Cover Photo by Douglas Salin
Cover design by E. Lynn Alexander

TABLE **Page**

For my grown children Morgan and Ed, so proud of you both. Also for Isaiah, Hyeji, Amy, Ruth, and Paul, for all of the reasons.

Finally, even though you are a bed hog, for Doug.

November dance shirt

Stitched
Wildflower petals and
Seasonal promises
Daily body shock
News the
Bombing the
Kidnapping the
Posturing
Peace is
Not a scale we should use to
Measure fuel and
Water
Fear can be slow poison we
Know something about
Forced relocation here if we
Put our hands up to it
Under a hunting moon we
Scavenge
Bonfire toffee and
Ginger a
Handful of
Almonds
Grated nutmeg
Mother's hand
Bombed building we
Learn to dance in
Bitter prayer smoke

Season of disqualification

Some remnant exiles
Some both
Dead and alive in a
Box halfway around the world
Nerveless cohorts with
Complicated motivations
Some die by inches some
Make hard choices and some will
Talk about them
Dogs
Struggling to please
Huntsman
Heart in a box there are
Survivors fed on
Panic fed on
Guilt and jealousy and don't they both
Translate as
Fear a
Phantom hunger the
News between
Advertisements for a
Holiday of overconsume

Road to November ends in

A locked
Gate a
Pile of the dead a
Judgment there are
Constant extinctions the
Fingers of a left hand can find a
Rock in the
Dust of any tragedy my rock is
Always a poem that
Might become soup in these times these
Extravagances of
Exquisite inedible the
Curio transformed the
Envelope of soup sent to the
Front and in this time of wonder the
Battle's edge is everywhere
Always behind each
Expensive and complicated
Sculpture of coffee and
Despair the war persists and my
Inelegant and workmanlike
Soup in
Carefully lettered and suspicious
Packages the
Handwriting a
Scaffold a
Confession a
Pile of feathers

This is not the welcome to the table I was

Taught

Beak digging into a ripe pear a
Prayer

Mary wrote prayers she
Worried about war
Some things pretend to be war and we
Talk about them like war but they are
Disguised

These are the knots I taught myself to tie
Particular in number and
Direction of crossing
This is a particular day for the
Telling of old stories

Beak
Digging into a ripe apple

Today walks
Disguised as war a
Pile of dead bison a
Fish trap a
Mass shooting on a river's bank

Fingers pass an imaginary line
Digging

Taught to walk the world

Ghosts we are
Thought to death thought
Dead by others and our
Cousins
Careful instructions
Careful rubrics for
Acceptance until the
Village boundary is
Moved again
How still can you be and
Keep breathing? Ever answer
Not still enough I
Wake strange walk
Strange through these social mazes
Sieves that
Belong to other people
Elsewhere
Bones
Salt
Abandoned songs
Checkout stand books I am
Spectacular in my
Inelegance

Neither of us is a lesson

Aging out of
Cloud spinning
Woeful stitching
Collecting language

Bread
Border
Captive
Limited
Closed

Hostage
Other hostage
Bomb
Rubble
Remnant

Water claws the stones soft under
Coast
Old song
Become forest
Become swallow

Embroidery pattern a symbol for
Home a memory of
Escape we
Wear our histories in our genes on our
Clothes we decorate each other with loss

Spells of peace are a constant

Working the
Circle we carry with us a
Dead child is a
Phantom limb a
Murder the
Poem of justification
Chalk dry a
Failed incantation a
Handful of teeth we find
While farming a
Handful of
Resurrection of
Parent's prayers
Prayers of dead parents a
Handful of
Baleful seeds there are those who
Feel the absent hand flexing
Reaching for
Peace a
Thing that needs
Tending
Always

Pretense of a shared language

Accurate translation but
Someone has to choose because
Words often mean
Self and
Opposite
Definite article
Difficult to define
Means an
Image that I expect
Indefinite article means
Yeah ok
You can add your idea too that
First sip that
Initial velocity the
Spin of parents and
Village and
Skip rope song
Child given what they want
Child made to make do the
Intention to understand the
Need to be understood

Shirt

Stitched with packets of love
Remembered it’s a rough affection to
Dance these prayers into chill
Mornings
What would Bill have done
What Mae
What story would Frank pull from his
Magic bag of
Endless stories the
Real wonders a matter of
Perspective and my stories my
Fugitive memories are not yours we will play
these
Endless games of
Pick up sticks
Train dexterity train an understanding of
Peace of
Disassemble of
Resent
Murder
Chipped flint ideas that are
All edges so that we can choose
We will train the children of the others
Often ourselves
How to hold dangerous ideas to
Do the most damage and
Wear our pain on new
Fine clothes
Picked out in careful stitches
As if we weren’t pulling our own
Graveyards over damp skin

Howl of old pain

One cup of butter half of a
Bomb casing the
Eggshell reference isn't lost here a
Clipping from the
Small tight curls behind my ears and the
Wind that sings through
Stones there are
Stairways in the woods the
Houses gone the houses
What will we leave behind in the
Mountains what
When we leave the forest
Each one taking a particular
Sacrifice yours is the
Hard breath the footfall the
Recipes of our
Foremothers a
Protection
Another spell we carry the
Weight the
Cry the wind the
Pieces of fallen ordinance their
Threat spent here or
Somewhere else

When the colonized are thought too dangerous

They are murdered
        Man with a funny nickname
        Neighbor who grows too many squash
Not
A people but
People
When the colonized are thought to be no threat
Stories are killed
Relationships of
        Tree to human
        Fish to flower and
People are murdered
One at a time and we are left to wonder
Is it a person or
A people taken

More countries celebrate independence

From colonial power
On this planet
We are linked in complication
Left with
Remainder colonies with their own story of
Grievance and the dances of the
Original people are forbidden then
Tolerated then
Fetish an amulet of someone's
Open mind you may
Live in the walls of a former home and the
Invasion might be called
Diaspora and we are
Linked in complication and some mornings
Are
Beautiful anyway and
In some places the knife is still at someone's
throat or the
Knife is put away and there is still a knife or
Ghost knives follow every action because
education can be a knife
Yes
We are more than our damage more than
What has been taken what is
Taken daily
Yes some days are still beautiful and we are
Sewn together
Edge to edge in complication

Some will never

Celebrate independence
Here in a month of First People's history
Spooling lists of
Violence the
Face of a four year old the
Kidnapped poet
I am here to tell you that
Relocation is not bloodless
I will tell you that I and mine have bled
We are the symbolic other and we have
Relocated
Blended
Loved and
Some of the family is thought to be one thing
Some another
Because
Synthesis is a difficult weight and
Someone will come to mark the lines
Gender lines
State lines
Skin and, membrane
Also borders
Some will never celebrate Independence
A new ceremonial dance of
Indifference

Here the steps go down

Into the
Wound the old one that
Doesn't bother to bleed sometimes that
Sings four songs at once the
Conditional freedoms a
New unbound book a
System of divination the
Ripe apple the
Cloak of self-deception
What can I hope for you a
Clean moment where others can see you we
People of glass an open
Door a history constructed of
Visible organs and
Deadly machines a
Bloody handprint a
Jar full of trophies and
Formaldehyde we can look into the
Fogged and preserved eyes of our
Mourned dead it may be that I will
Make flowers from the
Shattered glass or
Find rare medicine growing here but
That will not be today

Another unbound book

Unstitched page
Pried from page because pages
Are easier to hide in games in
Birthday cards
Sacred buildings
Always temporary
Taken to stones and
Fragments
Sewn into our hems
Shell casings
Buttons cut from the
Uniforms of the dead
Memento mori these
Horrible
Greed induced
Harvests and more
Obscured histories
When there they were the
Whole time in
Cells in
Blood

More mornings defining the human

A score
On the pain measuring tools
Some of them posted next to
Stock market numbers
Some of them part of
Stock market numbers
Some of them fingerprints
Some combed from nucleotides
Sorted and sifted
Some a thought experiment
Captive
Status unknown
Somewhere in the mythology of boxes

Tall ship into the bay

Did it look like a world was changing
Spell of unwilling transformation and
Even if these stories are told as fables the
Evidence is everywhere visible the
Lumpy mending stitches along
Every mark on the map
Across every tradition of
Gathering
Managing
Take anything with gold
Anything with silver any
Unusual curio'd artifact or
Food crop or
Seedpod the
Patterned fur the
Unpeople of this
Misreportedly unpeopled set of places

Pick the symbols carefully

We will
Tattoo them on our skin during the
Shattering we are become
Pebbles then
Breadcrumbs we are
Breadcrumbs finding our way home
We are the
Kaleidoscope and the microscope
We are
Removed
Removed
Scattered
Home is one another we set out on the
Long
Road

Lower the window

Breathe in this valley of
Garlic and flood these
Voluntary travels I used to
Avoid a
Genetic memory and
Don't we wander now
Heading south
Heading east that has to be symbolic doesn't it
Small planet we are
Always chasing water somehow the
Legacy fear the
Habit of hiding
Habit of the closed house and this
Valley we have traced the water here
Know the seeping hillside the
Reservoir the
Ghosts on the road
Fire roads and
Glassless buildings turn
South and watch the weather on the mountains
Over the mountains
Get the notes in order
Instructions for being a
Scrap
Directions for navigating a
Canyon the
Name for this kind of wind
Cycle of resurrection
Frayed edges

How much of identity is memory

Know the symbol not the meaning the
Hand cannot translate for the
Other hand and this
Genetic symbolism all
Arcs and confluences water
Storm water running
Sluicing wounds
Again the
Spasms
Unpredictable high tides
Low tides
Regional mispronunciations a
Balm for an
Unnoticed bruise I am a
Bruise of bruises a
Leaning in to the violence
Vintage the
Sound track the
Taste of carob the
Pillows on the floor and these
Astonishing pink and orange
Mornings

Today may be the day I

Shatter
Collection of engineered
Crush points and
Tempered glass
Moment where each
Individual piece and
Belief just
Comes apart in cartoon
Perfection and
Falls
From the top down
Into a polite and
Appropriate pile socially
Acceptable and
Expected assaults
Skin taut as
Nightfall the
Violence of untranslated
Expectation the
Residual lateral violence the
Freight of holding the keys the
Cynical offer of one
Possible road to
Peace and all they ask is that you
Be someone else

Whichever system

Continual shallow cuts they ask
Aren't you more than your damage
        A cut
We've taught you to write
        Another cut
Be grateful to be noticed
        The knife at your wrist
You are the next thing to be harvested
        Another young woman vanishes
You don't know what it is to be
Colonized
        Translations are tricky so I will decide
But you survived
        You may live in the walls of your old
house

One more last minute performance

To pay the bills
Stare up the ladder the
One that leads out of the wound you
Know you will climb it like
Walking out of the desert
Walking west
Walking the delicate light on
Calm
Pacific water the path is
Ephemeral
You climb it anyway
Muscle sore you climb it
Let the comments fall like
Flint shards
Pale as the skin on your wrists and in the
Daze hybrid genes it's hard to know
Whose skin
Yours now like the sign off to a letter it's not
All misery but you can't find the
Cord to pull the one oh
Here the one that pulls the
Shades closed

Freedom talk continues

Evidence of poets past the
Dance the
Music box spin
All magnets and
Illusion of life the
Battle for the creation story we
Whispering in corners
Isolated in our own
Gestures the
Unacceptable the
Preferably forgotten the
Community you walk away from the
Community you are left with the
Water declared a privilege walking
Upstream
Walking into the
Sacred lake wondering if it's
Quiet
There

That morning

Your own heart found in the
Trunk of a tree
Absorbed at some point or
Put there for safe keeping
Readjust the dance shirt
Only slightly worn the
Months designated for the other
Performance
Breakfast
Performance window
Prism rocking slightly and all of the
Small rainbows
Flick in and out of view
Make no mistake
They are always there the
Thick indifferent slices of
Light as you
Kabuki identity in
Shards like
Flaked obsidian or
Shop windows in the 30s or
Shop windows last week a
Spill pile of metaphor

Words may cut your fingers

No
Will cut your fingers
Can you sing the story
Wordless the
Shells hit the sink
Right near the drain what
Spells
Stories will I
Knit into the blankets for the children
How many
Which ones you can
Tell them
The world will
Change it is
Changing and you may
Shock
Pulling yourself upright again
It happens
Breathe as deeply as you can
Cry when you feel it
Reread as often as you want
Shells hit the sink
Large and small pieces we
Feed the community

Strawberry prints

On paper towel little
Red mouths
If you could be a
Vampire if you could
Bake the meat pies if you could
Set the beads in lines to
Tell a specific bird like a
Fable a
Frog like a
Rainstorm the
Last shivers of this
Clench of November add the
Paprika the cinnamon
Misunderstood names and
Confetti thought a
Time of choreographed food and
Curated emotion
More cinnamon
Lean back on a memory of
Grandpa and card games
Card games late at night the
Heater and
Light from the stove

Daylight still

Choppy but
Settling
Neither sung nor
Unsung my
Fear of heights kicks in the
Raven calls me from the
Power lines
Has brought a friend
Dance shirt back in the closet
Stored like any number of other
Identities
Tasks like rungs of a ladder like
Steps to an absent door like
Finding
Balance

New minted story with

Just that chill and stripe
Rain and new paint
Tortoise shell frames the
Belief in nothing or everything is
Tradition
These old scraps of self
Stitched over new there is
Wear left in them
Some wear left

Keen a

Cry an
Edge and we fold and we
Press and we
Cradle one set of
Memory decorations a
Shirt
Orange as new coal a
Continued brace against it's all
Cease fire and hot war in
Strobe patterns on the insides of my
Eyelids a
Geometry of anxiety and
Firing synapses
Someone's thought experiment a baby in the
Box the
Beloved injured or dead or
Both something about the heft of a
Bomb the
Freight of
Panic

Kim Shuck served four years as San Francisco's Poet Laureate. Her organizing and influence over the Bay Area poetry community simply cannot be quantified.

She is the author of *Pick A Garnet To Sleep In, Noodle Rant Tangent, What Unseen Thing Blows Wishes Across My Surface, Exile Heart, Murdered Missing, Deer Trails, Rabbit Stories* and of course the legendary *Clouds Running In.*

Photo by Douglas A. Salin

MORE TITLES FROM COLLAPSE PRESS

www.collapsepress.com

Unit of Agency
By Richard Loranger

deathaiku
by Missy Church

Splinters
by Han Raschka

Find Me in the Iris
by E. Lynn Alexander

four crescents
by Norm Mattox

Thawing: A Poetic Memoir
by Taneesh Kaur

19th Street Station Volume 2
by Paul Corman-Roberts

Headless
by Sean Hanrahan

For The Duration
By Heather Flescher

Letters for the End Times Volume 1 (2023)

Letters for the End Times Volume 2 (2024)

Made in the USA
Coppell, TX
09 June 2026

79941918R00024